ANOTHER COUNTRY

3

PRISONER AND STATESWOMAN

4

A NOBLE
CHILDHOOD

1

Noble Birth

Above: This medieval illustration shows a troubadour strolling through the countryside. Troubadours were poet-musicians who wrote and sang love poems that were popular in the 1100s.

Previous page: Peasants harvest crops and shear sheep in front of Poitiers Castle in a detail from a 15th-century illustrated manuscript.

Eleanor of Aquitaine lived more than 800 years ago. At a time when women had few rights, she became queen of France and England, and one of the most powerful women of her time.

Eleanor was born in 1122 in the duchy of Aquitaine, a huge region in the southwest of what is now France. She came from a privileged and noble background. Eleanor's father was William X, duke of Aquitaine. He was a tall, imposing man, who was often quick to quarrel. Eleanor's mother was called Aenor. Historians know very little about Aenor, but she was the daughter of a strong-willed woman called Dangerosa, the viscountess of Châtellerault. Eleanor had a younger sister, Petronilla, and a brother, William Aigret.

Eleanor's grandfather died when she was about four or five, but his adventures made a strong impression on her life. He was William IX, duke of Aquitaine. Like her father, he was powerful and wealthy. He was also a cultured man who wrote music and poetry that Eleanor would have heard when she was a child. He was probably the first *troubadour*, or poet-musician.

1094
Eleanor's grandfather, William IX, marries Philippa. Their son, William (b. 1099), will be Eleanor's father.

1095
Pope Urban II urges European Christians to take Jerusalem from Muslim Turks.

Eleanor's grandfather divorced his first wife, Ermengarde, then married again, to a woman named Philippa. They had seven children, one of whom was Eleanor's father. Her grandfather then fell in love with Dangerosa, who was also married. He kidnapped her and brought her to his castle. In 1121, his son married Dangerosa's daughter from her previous marriage, Aenor. Eleanor was their first child.

Below: Eleanor's home was the great palace at Poitiers in the duchy of Aquitaine.

Eleanor's birth

There is very little information about Eleanor's early life. Historians do not know exactly where or when she was born. She was probably born in April 1122, either in Poitiers or the castle of Ombrière in Bordeaux. She was named alia-Aenor, which is Latin for "the other Aenor," or Eleanor in English.

1096
Thousands of European Christians travel to the Holy Land on the First Crusade.

1099
The First Crusaders seize Jerusalem.

Aquitaine

Eleanor grew up in Aquitaine. She always loved the duchy. It was a sophisticated region and the source of her family's wealth and importance. When Eleanor was born, her family's domains stretched from the Loire River in the north to the Pyrenees mountains on the Spanish border in the south, and the mountains of the Massif Central in the east to the Atlantic Ocean in the west.

WALES
ENGLAND
London   Rochester
Thames   Canterbury
Salisbury   Winchester
English Channel
FLANDERS
VEXIN
Rouen
NORMANDY   Paris   CHAMPAGNE
BRITTANY
Chartres   Vitry
MAINE   ANJOU   FRANCE
Fontevrault
Atlantic Ocean   Chinon   Vézelay
POITOU   Mirabeau   BURGUNDY
Poitiers   Loire
AQUITAINE   Cluny
Limoges
Angoulême   Clermont
Gaillard
Bordeaux   Massif Central
GASCONY   Garonne   TOULOUSE
SPAIN   Pyrenees

Aquitaine
France
Border of French influence

Aquitaine was a warm, fertile region containing mountains and forests, meadows, vineyards, and olive groves. The duchy had plenty of villages, farms, small walled cities, castles, monasteries, and ports.

Left: The map shows France and England as they were in the 1100s. It includes Eleanor's homeland of Aquitaine and the kingdom of France. It shows many of the French and English places Eleanor visited during her life. France was then a small kingdom, surrounded by counties and duchies that often fought each other. Aquitaine was the largest.

1100

The great abbey of Fontevrault is founded, with money given by William IX.

1121

Eleanor's father marries Aenor, the daughter of Dangerosa.

Eleanor's ancestors had ruled Aquitaine for 300 years. Their home was the castle of Poitiers, an ancient walled area and capital of Poitou, Aquitaine's most important county. The dukes of Aquitaine were powerful, but the king of France was their overlord. They owed him allegiance, although they often rebelled. France then was only a very small kingdom. Eleanor's father, as duke of Aquitaine, had more land and vassals (nobles who owed him allegiance) than Louis VI, who was king of France at the time.

The people of Aquitaine were known for being brave, witty, and independent. Members of their nobility lived a more luxurious lifestyle than those in the north. The noblewomen of Aquitaine had often had a little more freedom than noblewomen in other parts of France. Eleanor heard stories of many strong-minded women from history, such as her grandmother, Dangerosa. These women made powerful role models.

Below: Aquitaine was a beautiful area with many castles and an ancient history. The Romans called it Aquitainia, meaning "land of waters," because of its many rivers.

1121
Louis VII, future king of France, is born. He is the second son of Louis VI, known as Louis the Fat.

1122
Eleanor of Aquitaine is born either in Poitiers or Bordeaux.

Medieval Society

The Middle Ages was a period in European history that lasted from the fifth century to the 15th century. It is also called the medieval period. Life was very different from today. People did not vote and there were no central governments—kings and nobles held the power, and land was the basis of wealth. In England and France, a system that historians call feudalism governed society. Kings gave land to nobles and knights, who promised to serve them. Europe was split into kingdoms, ruled by royalty; duchies, ruled by dukes; and smaller counties, ruled by counts. There were few towns, and most people lived in the countryside. But by Eleanor's time, towns and trade were developing.

KING

NOBLES

KNIGHTS

PEASANTS

FEUDAL SOCIETY

The king was at the top of medieval society. He granted land, called fiefs, to powerful nobles, called vassals, who swore allegiance and agreed to serve him. Vassals granted land to lesser nobles and knights, who swore allegiance to them and provided military service. Knights were the warriors of feudal society. They were obliged to serve their lords for 40 days every year.

Left: A medieval knight swears an oath of loyalty.

Right: A peasant woman working in the fields. Peasants were at the very bottom of medieval society. Their land, homes, food, and animals belonged to their lord. In exchange for working the land, they could keep some of the food they produced. Peasant women raised children, spun wool, and labored in fields.

Left: Women had few rights in the medieval world, but noblewomen (left) had a little more power than peasant women. They could inherit and own land. But when a woman married, she lost all rights over her property, which went to her husband. A woman's role was to honor, obey, and serve her husband. However, many noblewomen ran households and family estates while their husbands were away fighting.

Above: Pope Urban II (1035–99) blesses a church in Cluny, France. In medieval Europe, Christianity ruled everyone's lives. The pope was the head of the church and was thought to be God's representative on Earth. He had the power to punish people by banning them from the church.

Life in the Great Hall

When Eleanor was a child she spent a lot of time in the castle at Poitiers. It was her family home and a mighty fortress. Poitiers Castle was already several centuries old when Eleanor was born. It stood high on a cliff and had thick stone walls capable of repelling the fiercest invaders. Soldiers stood guard on the high walls around the castle, called ramparts.

The family lived in apartments in the Maubergeonne Tower, which had been built by Eleanor's ancestor, William VII. There are no detailed descriptions of how Eleanor spent her childhood, but life in the palace would have been exciting, with visitors coming and going and messengers bringing news from around Aquitaine.

In the summer, Eleanor and Petronilla played in the beautiful palace gardens, which were full of fruit trees. In the evenings, everyone gathered in the great hall to eat and be entertained.

Left: The nobility enjoyed lavish banquets, or feasts. Meat included venison, swan, goose, crane, and even peacock. Sauces were highly spiced. They ate lobsters and oysters, and a variety of sweet puddings and fruits, all washed down with wine. People ate with knives and their hands because there were no forks.

1125
Eleanor's sister, Aelith, is born. She was usually known as Petronilla, which is Latin for "Younger Sister."

1126
Rochester Castle is built in England, one of many great buildings to be constructed during the 12th century.

Right: A medieval conjurer produces a rabbit. Acrobats, jugglers, and musicians entertained not just in noble courts but also at festivals and feasts.

supne dispensationis insinuans: de ele[...]
[...] percussione intulit dicens

A large fire in a huge fireplace provided heat. Clean rushes covered the bare wooden floors. Candles were used for light.

Poitiers was the cultural center of western Europe. Eleanor would have seen skilled entertainers, many of whom traveled from castle to castle throughout Europe. There would have been jugglers and acrobats, and puppet masters who worked puppets called marionettes. Eleanor would have listened to musicians who played stringed instruments, flutes, and small drums, called tabors. There would also have been minstrels, called *jongleurs*, storytellers, and troubadours, who sang about women and love. When Eleanor was very young, she would have heard her grandfather singing the love poems and songs he had written himself. She developed a love of music that lasted her whole life.

Castle hygiene

There were no flush toilets in medieval Europe. Instead, people used what was called a privy. Most castle privies consisted of a wooden or stone seat over a long shaft that emptied into the castle moat. People took baths in wooden tubs, which could be moved near the fire for warmth.

1126

Averroës is born in Muslim-ruled Córdoba, Spain. He becomes one of the greatest Islamic thinkers.

1126–27

Eleanor's brother, William Aigret, is born. Historians are not sure of the exact date of his birth.

A Lively Girl

Eleanor was a bright, intelligent, and lively young girl. She was also well educated, which was unusual for the time. The majority of girls in the Middle Ages did not have much formal education. There were few schools—and they were not intended for girls.

Girls were supposed to learn how to be obedient wives and good mothers. They needed to know how to run a home, but reading and writing were not considered important skills for most of them.

Eleanor, however, had a privileged upbringing. Unlike many other girls, she was carefully educated and taught a range of different skills. She was quick-witted, strong-willed, and probably rather spoiled. From her mother, and perhaps her grandmother too, she learned traditional women's skills such as sewing and embroidery. She was taught how to run a huge household. Aenor would have taught many young girls, not just her own daughters. It was the custom for the daughters of noble families to be sent to wealthier households for instruction.

Above: Medieval children playing blind man's bluff. Children in the Middle Ages played games like hide and seek, chanted rhymes, and played with toys.

1127
In England, the barons accept Matilda, daughter of King Henry I, as heir to the English throne.

February 10, 1127
Eleanor's grandfather, William IX, dies. Eleanor's father becomes William X, duke of Aquitaine.

Above: A woman and man riding together. The man has a hawk on his arm. Girls of the nobility learned to ride at an early age. Hunting with hawks was a popular sport for noblewomen.

How we know

Since Eleanor probably could not write, she did not keep a diary or write personal letters. She would have used a scribe for official letters. Most of what we know about her life comes from people who wrote about her, sometimes much later. In the 1170s, the troubadour Richard le Poitevan said Eleanor was "reared with an abundance of all delights, living in the bosom of wealth."

Eleanor was also taught how to read Latin, probably by the castle clergyman. Latin was the language of learning. She also learned to read *Provençal*, a type of French spoken in Aquitaine. Reading and writing were seen as separate skills in the Middle Ages, and many people who were taught to read could not actually write. Historians think this was the case with Eleanor.

Eleanor always loved the arts, especially poetry and literature. She played the harp and enjoyed singing and dancing. She learned to play board games, such as chess, which had recently arrived in Europe from the East. She was also taught to ride and to hunt with birds of prey called falcons that could be trained to hunt small creatures. She rode well and liked to ride with her legs on either side of the horse, rather than sidesaddle, which was how most women rode at the time.

1128

Matilda, daughter of Henry I, king of England, marries Geoffrey Plantagenet, the count of Anjou.

1128

The pope formally acknowledges the Knights Templar, a group of soldier monks who fought in the crusades.

TEENAGE
QUEEN

fais ⁊ la vie du Roy loys le gros
Cy commencent les fais du Roy loys filz du

A Traveling Court

Like other medieval rulers, Eleanor's father had a traveling court, and Eleanor traveled extensively with her father around Aquitaine. From these travels she was able to learn how the duchy was governed. Every year, her father gathered up his family and rode through his domain to check on his vassals and to collect taxes or crops owed to him. Eleanor went with him, as did the whole household, including scribes, knights, musicians, chaplains, clerks, cooks, and other servants.

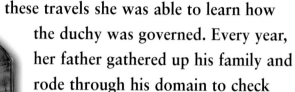

Above: Louis II (1377–1417), duke of Anjou, enters Paris. Monarchs and rulers, like Eleanor's father, traveled through their lands accompanied by nobles, knights, and servants.

Previous page: This medieval illustration shows two scenes from Eleanor's life: her marriage to Louis (left) and her journey to the Holy Land (right).

The duke's household traveled from one end of Aquitaine to another, setting up court in castles and keeps around the duchy. William's vassals provided food and lodging. Eleanor saw her father conducting business in every part of Aquitaine. They often stayed in the palace of Ombrière in Bordeaux. Here, Eleanor watched her father receive his vassals, sign documents or petitions, settle disputes, and administer the duchy.

1129

Eleanor's name appears on a document for the first time. She signs her name with a cross, because she cannot write.

1130

Eleanor's mother, Aenor, and brother, William Aigret, die.

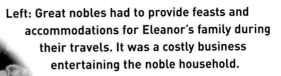

Left: Great nobles had to provide feasts and accommodations for Eleanor's family during their travels. It was a costly business entertaining the noble household.

Eleanor had an official role. When she was about seven, she witnessed a document granting privileges to monks in the Abbey of Montierneuf, where her grandfather was buried. She wrote a cross in ink next to her name, probably using a quill pen.

Eleanor's father was impulsive and quarrelsome. In 1130, he quarreled with the church over who should be the next pope. Eleanor's father supported Anacletus II, a cardinal who was challenging the existing pope, Innocent II. William drove all the churchmen who supported Innocent out of Aquitaine. As a result, Bernard de Clairvaux, a powerful and influential cleric, banned, or excommunicated, him from the church.

Also in 1130, Eleanor's mother and little brother died, leaving Eleanor and her sister as the sole surviving children. Her brother, as a boy, had been her father's heir, but now Eleanor was next in line to inherit the duchy of Aquitaine.

Punished by the church

Excommunication meant a person was banned from the Catholic church and could not take part in church services. It was a harsh punishment—the church said that the soul of an excommunicated person was damned.

1131

Louis, the second son of King Louis VI of France, becomes heir to the French throne when his elder brother dies.

1133

Eleanor's uncle, Raymond of Poitiers, goes to the Holy Land to become ruler of Antioch.

Wealthy Heiress

After their mother's death, Eleanor and her sister were left to their own devices. Always argumentative and impatient, Eleanor's father was caught up in his own problems.

Aquitaine was rarely at peace: some of William's vassals were showing signs of rebelling against him. There was also no sign of an end to his quarrels with the church. In 1135, when Eleanor was 13, William stormed into a church where Bernard de Clairvaux was celebrating mass. Bernard confronted the excommunicated William, who suffered a seizure or fit and collapsed. When William recovered, he repented for quarreling with the pope. William also became depressed. He wanted a son to inherit his lands, and decided to marry again.

He chose Emma, countess of Limoges. She held power over Limousin, a small province of Aquitaine.

Left: This 14th-century manuscript shows King Louis VI of France (1081–1137) watching builders work. He was known as Louis the Fat because he was very large. His first son died in 1131 and his second son, Louis, became his heir.

1135
William X makes peace with the church. He founds an abbey as an act of penance.

1136
William X proposes to Emma, countess of Limoges, but she is kidnapped and married to the count of Angoulême.

Nobles in Limousin wanted to stop William from gaining more power over them. They kidnapped Emma and forced her to marry the count of Angoulême. Surprisingly, William did not fight back.

In 1137, William decided to make a pilgrimage to the church of St. James at Santiago de Compostela in Spain. Eleanor and Petronilla went with him as far as Bordeaux, where William left them with the archbishop, one of his loyal vassals. He told Eleanor he would return wearing a cockleshell badge, the symbol of St. James. With just a few knights and servants, William arrived in Spain. There he became ill, and, realizing he was dying, he bequeathed Aquitaine to Eleanor and put the duchy and Eleanor under the protection of King Louis VI of France. Then William died. Back in Bordeaux, Eleanor was now duchess of Aquitaine, Poitou, and Gascony, and a wealthy landowner.

Left: Medieval women putting on their finery. By the age of 15, Eleanor was very beautiful. She loved to wear elegant clothes and jewelry.

A pilgrim's badge

Bands of pilgrims were a common sight during the Middle Ages. Many people went on pilgrimages—long journeys by land and sea—to places such as Rome or Compostela, where there were sacred relics. They hoped to receive forgiveness for sins, or miracle cures for illness. Those who went to Compostela wore a metal cockleshell-shaped badge.

1136
William commands the nobles of Aquitaine to swear loyalty, or fealty, to Eleanor.

April 10, 1137
William X dies while on pilgrimage. He is buried at the cathedral in Compostela, Spain.

Marriage

Eleanor's life changed completely after her father died. Almost immediately, Louis VI arranged for Eleanor to marry his son, who was also named Louis. Eleanor was 15 years old and Louis was 16.

Louis VI was seriously ill near Paris when news reached him that his most powerful vassal, William X, had died. Swiftly, he made plans for his son Louis to marry Eleanor. Gaining control of Aquitaine would increase France's land and influence. Eleanor was at Ombrière, heavily guarded in case an ambitious noble tried to kidnap her. We do not know how she felt about her father's death or the marriage plans.

In June, young Louis left Paris for Aquitaine. With him went 500 knights; great lords; the king's chief minister, Abbot Suger; and mules laden with tents, cooking equipment, gold, and jewels. Their journey took about a month. It was hot, and the huge procession often traveled by night.

Left: Statues of Eleanor and Louis in Chartres Cathedral, France. The young couple were very different. Louis was indecisive and deeply religious. Eleanor was confident and bold.

April 1137
Eleanor inherits Aquitaine, Poitou, and Gascony. She is the wealthiest heiress in western Europe.

June 18, 1137
Louis VI sends his son, Prince Louis, to Bordeaux to marry Eleanor.

Louis reached Ombrière in July and set up camp near the Garonne River. With its colorful pavilions and many knights, the royal camp was a glorious sight. Louis was ferried across the river to the castle, and Eleanor met her husband-to-be for the first time. A few days later, they were married in the cathedral of St. André in Bordeaux.

After the wedding, Eleanor and Louis traveled through Bordeaux, passing houses hung with tapestries and banners. There was a wedding banquet at Ombrière. The couple then went to Poitiers, where celebrations continued and Eleanor's vassals arrived to swear allegiance.

Not all of Eleanor's vassals were pleased, and some stayed away. One was William de Lezay. Louis and his knights set off to punish him. There was a violent confrontation and many of the rebels were slaughtered.

An arranged marriage
Parents from noble families arranged marriages to increase their power. When Eleanor's father died, Louis VI was her overlord and chose his son to become her husband.

Above: Eleanor gave this rock crystal and gold vase to Louis as a wedding present. The vase is the only one of Eleanor's possessions to survive. It is in the Louvre museum in Paris.

June 29, 1137
Prince Louis and his retinue arrive in Limoges. They reach the Ombrière Palace on July 11.

July 25, 1137
Eleanor and Louis are married in Bordeaux. They are made duchess and duke of Aquitaine.

Queen of France

In August 1137, Eleanor and Louis left Aquitaine for Paris. News came that Louis VI had died. Suddenly, Eleanor's husband was king of France, and she—a teenager—was queen.

Below: This medieval stained-glass window from Chartres Cathedral shows carpenters at work. Many great cathedrals were built in France during the 12th and 13th centuries. They had soaring spires and arched stained-glass windows.

Eleanor was crowned queen on Christmas Day, 1137. Her new home was the Cité Palace in Paris. It was a grim tower, with small, drafty rooms. Her new husband was devoted to her, but he was even more interested in religion. For high-spirited Eleanor, life was rather dull after Aquitaine. She had brought noble ladies and troubadours with her, and tried to recreate the liveliness of Aquitaine in her Paris home. The French criticized her extravagant lifestyle.

Marriage to Eleanor brought problems for Louis. Back in Poitiers, some of Eleanor's nobles rebelled against French control. Eleanor's sister, Petronilla, became involved with a married count, Raoul of Vermandois. Raoul's wife was the sister to Count Theobold of Champagne. Louis arranged a divorce for Raoul so he could marry Petronilla. Theobold was furious.

August 1137
Louis VI dies. Eleanor's husband, Louis, succeeds him as Louis VII, king of France.

December 25, 1137
Eleanor is crowned queen of France.

He protested to the pope, who excommunicated Petronilla and Raoul. In revenge, Louis led an army against Theobold. His forces attacked the count's castle in Vitry. They launched flaming arrows at the castle, which was wooden and caught fire. Terrified people sought safety in a wooden church nearby and were burned alive when that caught fire as well.

Eleanor tried to bargain with the powerful Bernard de Clairvaux. She offered to persuade Louis to make peace if Bernard would encourage the pope to lift her sister's excommunication. Bernard ordered her to stop interfering in state affairs; her duty was to be an obedient wife and produce sons. Cleverly, Eleanor pleaded that her greatest wish was indeed to have children. She won his sympathy and he helped to arrange a peace treaty.

Below: The abbey of St. Denis, near Paris, today. Abbot Suger had this splendid abbey built to replace a much older church. In 1144, Eleanor and Louis attended its dedication.

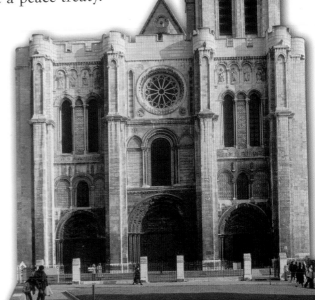

A palace makeover

Eleanor changed the royal palace in Paris. She ordered slit windows to be widened to let in more light, and had a huge fireplace built. She also introduced table manners: tablecloths and napkins were used and pages had to wash their hands before serving food.

1142–43
Louis wages war against the count of Champagne. He suffers remorse when 1,000 people are burned alive.

1145
Eleanor's first surviving child, Marie, is born. Eleanor had been pregnant before, but the baby died at birth.

Crusades

In 1095, Pope Urban II called on Christians to march to the Holy Land and take control of Jerusalem from the Muslim Turks. Then, just as today, Jerusalem was a holy place to Christians, as well as to Muslims and Jews. Thousands of Christians from all over Europe and all walks of life responded and set off on what became known as the First Crusade. Between 1096 and 1270, there were eight crusades. They took their name from the Latin word *crux*, meaning "cross," which every crusader wore. The First Crusaders captured Jerusalem and set up Christian kingdoms in the Holy Land. These kingdoms were Jerusalem, Antioch, Edessa, and Tripoli. The kingdoms came under constant attack and, in 1187, the Muslim leader Saladin recaptured Jerusalem. Other crusades followed, with Jerusalem being regained and lost once more. In 1291, the last Christian stronghold, Acre, fell to the Muslims.

Right: This map shows Europe and the Holy Land in the 12th century. Crusaders, including Eleanor, traveled by land or sea from Europe to the Middle East. It was a long and dangerous journey. Many died on the way.

ENGLAND
London
St. Denis
Paris
FRANCE
Poitiers
AQUITAINE
Santiago de Compostela
NAVARRE
Pyrenees
CASTILE
SPAIN

TIMELINE

1096–99 FIRST CRUSADE
Christians capture Jerusalem and set up Christian kingdoms on the Syrian coast.
1147–49 SECOND CRUSADE
Louis VII and Conrad III of Germany lead the crusade, which is a failure. Eleanor goes with Louis.
1189–92 THIRD CRUSADE
Christians take Acre, but Muslims keep Jerusalem. Eleanor's son, Richard I, is one of the leaders of the crusade.

1202–04 FOURTH CRUSADE
Crusaders loot Constantinople (Istanbul).
1212 CHILDREN'S CRUSADE
Thousands of children cross Europe. Most die of hunger or disease. Many are sold into slavery.
1217–21 FIFTH CRUSADE
Crusaders capture and lose land in Egypt.
1228–29 SIXTH CRUSADE
A truce is declared.
1248–54 LOUIS IX'S FIRST CRUSADE
The French capture Damietta briefly.
1270 LOUIS IX'S SECOND CRUSADE
Louis IX of France dies on crusade.

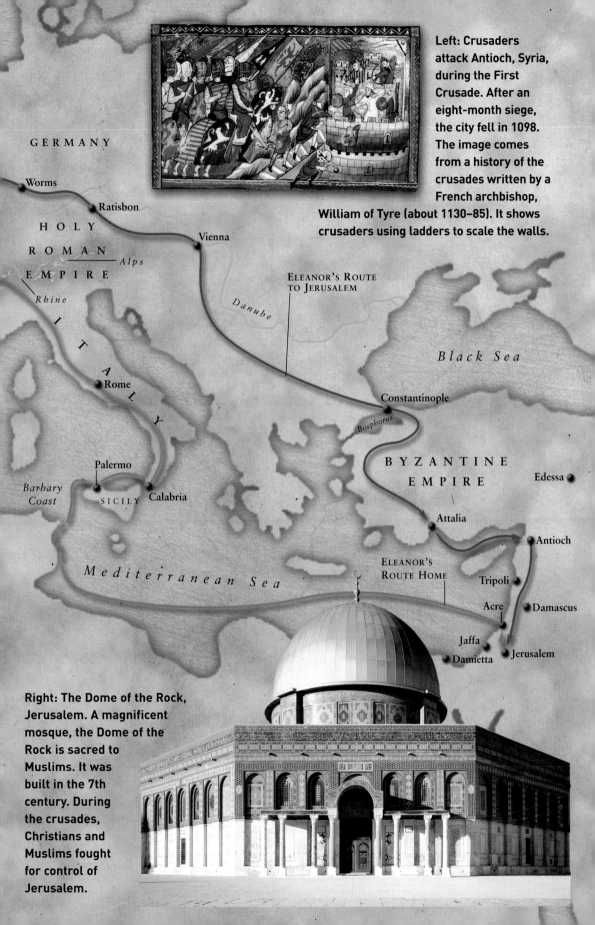

Left: Crusaders attack Antioch, Syria, during the First Crusade. After an eight-month siege, the city fell in 1098. The image comes from a history of the crusades written by a French archbishop, William of Tyre (about 1130–85). It shows crusaders using ladders to scale the walls.

GERMANY

Worms

Ratisbon

HOLY
ROMAN
EMPIRE

Alps

Vienna

Rhine

ELEANOR'S ROUTE
TO JERUSALEM

Danube

Black Sea

I
T
A
L
Y

Rome

Constantinople

Bosphorus

Palermo

*Barbary
Coast*

SICILY   Calabria

BYZANTINE
EMPIRE

Edessa

Mediterranean Sea

Attalia

Antioch

ELEANOR'S
ROUTE HOME

Tripoli

Acre   Damascus

Jaffa

Damietta   Jerusalem

Right: The Dome of the Rock, Jerusalem. A magnificent mosque, the Dome of the Rock is sacred to Muslims. It was built in the 7th century. During the crusades, Christians and Muslims fought for control of Jerusalem.

Crusading Queen

In 1146, the pope called for a crusade. Muslim Turks had seized Edessa and were threatening Christian-held Jerusalem and Antioch. Louis decided to lead the Holy War, and Eleanor announced that she would go too.

Below: Bernard de Clairvaux preaching the crusade to a huge number of people at Vézelay, in 1146. So many people demanded a cross—the emblem of the crusade—that Bernard cut his white robe into strips to make cloth crosses.

Eleanor was 24 and she had a young daughter, but life in Paris was boring and a crusade would be a big adventure. When Bernard de Clairvaux preached the crusade at Vézelay, she and Louis took the cross with enthusiasm. She went to Aquitaine, where she recruited 1,000 of her vassals and knights, the largest fighting force recruited from any one region. She also raised money by organizing tournaments and granting privileges to religious houses in exchange for gold.

June 11, 1147
Eleanor and Louis leave St. Denis on the Second Crusade at the head of a huge army.

October 3–16, 1147
Eleanor and Louis stay in Constantinople, the glittering capital of the Byzantine Empire.

Right: This metal engraving shows crusaders traveling by ship to the Holy Land. It was created in the 12th century and is found in St. Mark's Basilica in Venice.

A likely story

It is said that Eleanor and her women rode through the crowds at Vézelay on white horses, dressed like women warriors called Amazons. They waved their swords and urged people to join the crusade. It is a colorful story but there is no proof it happened.

In 1147, Eleanor and Louis set off from St. Denis with a vast army of some 100,000 people. Their daughter stayed at home. Eleanor rode near the front with her vassals and luggage. With her traveled other noblewomen and 300 women of lesser rank. Louis and his soldiers brought up the rear.

Traveling between 10 and 20 miles (15–30 km) a day, the huge procession wound its way through Germany and Hungary. In October, they reached Constantinople, now called Istanbul. Eleanor had never seen anything like this city, with its exotic spices, tiled pathways, and glorious fountains.

The crusaders crossed the Bosphorus into Asia. Traveling was difficult, the weather worsened, and food supplies ran low. Eleanor traded jewelry for food. Louis decided to take the crusade over the mountains to Antioch. Turkish forces harassed them constantly. Eleanor and her women traveled in horse-drawn litters with thick leather curtains for protection.

January 1148
Eleanor arrives in Attalia, Turkey

March 19–28, 1148
Eleanor and Louis stay in Antioch with Eleanor's uncle. Louis forces Eleanor to travel to Jerusalem.

Above: This 15th-century painting by Jean Fouquet portrays the entry into Constantinople of Louis VII along with the king of Germany, Conrad III (1093–1152).

Disaster struck on a mountain pass when Eleanor and her vassals ignored instructions and went ahead to find a better place to camp, leaving the main army dangerously exposed. Turkish forces made a surprise attack and Louis' army suffered terrible losses. More than 7,000 crusaders were killed. The French blamed Eleanor and her vassals for having left them unprotected.

Louis changed his mind and decided to continue to Antioch by sea. He and Eleanor set sail from the port of Attalia. Three weeks later, after a stormy and dangerous voyage that should only have taken three days, they arrived in Antioch. Eleanor's uncle, Raymond, ruler of Antioch, came to greet them. Eleanor was thrilled. Raymond was 36, a handsome, decisive warrior, quite different from Eleanor's husband. Eleanor and Louis stayed in Raymond's palace and were entertained lavishly. Raymond and Eleanor spent time together and there was gossip; Louis became jealous. Raymond wanted Louis' army to help him attack Edessa. Louis refused and he told Eleanor that they were leaving for Jerusalem. There was an argument and Eleanor threatened to stay and put her forces at Raymond's service.

Early summer 1149
Eleanor and Louis leave Acre in separate ships. Eleanor is captured briefly. Her ship is blown off course.

July–August 1149
Eleanor joins Louis in Calabria. They leave overland for France.

She was tired of her weak husband. She told him that she wanted a divorce. Louis acted swiftly. His soldiers seized Eleanor by force, and they left secretly for Jerusalem. Eleanor was furious and disgraced.

Finally, they arrived in Jerusalem, where Louis did penance. Against all advice, he attacked the Muslim-held city of Damascus. It was a serious misjudgment because Damascus was friendly to Christians, but Louis was greedy for land and did not understand the situation. His forces besieged the city but were forced to retreat, with considerable loss of life. The crusade was a failure: it had done nothing to strengthen the Christian position in the Holy Land. The French were humiliated and their soldiers were deserting.

In 1149, Eleanor and Louis began the long journey home. They sailed from Acre in separate ships, bound for southern Italy. While at sea, Greek forces attacked, intending to take Eleanor and Louis hostage. Eleanor's ship was captured briefly, but Sicilian forces drove off the attackers. Storms drove the ships apart and Eleanor was possibly shipwrecked on the Barbary Coast. She rejoined Louis in Calabria, Italy, and they continued overland.

The journey home was slow and Eleanor was often ill. Louis and Eleanor stayed with the pope in Rome and told him of their marriage problems. He refused a divorce and urged them to resolve their differences. Eleanor and Louis finally arrived in Paris, nearly two and a half years after leaving.

> *"Gracious, lovely, the embodiment of charm... one meet [suitable] to crown the state of any king..."*
> **A description of Eleanor by Bernard de Ventadour, troubadour, 1153**

October 9–10, 1149
Eleanor and Louis visit the pope in Rome, Italy. Their marriage is unhappy. The pope urges them to make up.

November 1149
Eleanor and Louis arrive back in Paris, France.

ANOTHER
COUNTRY

Divorce and Remarriage

Eleanor and Louis returned to Paris during a bitter winter. They quarreled frequently and Eleanor still wanted a divorce. She said she had married a monk, not a king. In 1150, Eleanor gave birth to a second daughter, but Louis really wanted a son and heir.

In Antioch, Eleanor had said their marriage was cursed. Now Louis began to think she was right. Abbot Suger tried to keep them together—the loss of Aquitaine would leave France weak—but many of Louis' nobles thought Eleanor meddled too much and wanted him to divorce her. After Suger died in 1152, Louis finally agreed to divorce.

Louis had other matters to settle. Two of his powerful vassals—Geoffrey, count of Anjou, and Geoffrey's son, Henry, duke of Normandy—were challenging his authority. Louis summoned them to Paris.

Previous page: A man looks adoringly at the woman he loves in this symbol of courtly love.

Left: Bishops grant Louis VII his divorce. The official grounds for the divorce were that Louis and Eleanor were too closely related— they were fourth cousins. Husbands and wives being related was not unusual, however. All the European royal houses were related to each other.

1150

Eleanor's second daughter, Alix, is born.

August 1151

Geoffrey of Anjou and his son Henry visit Eleanor and Louis in Paris.

He demanded that Henry should pay him homage—a formal oath of allegiance. At first, father and son stormed out. Later, they returned and Henry pledged allegiance, placing his hands between Louis' palms.

Eleanor was attracted to Henry. At 17, he was 11 years younger than she was, and he was a forceful, handsome young man. She decided that, once divorced, she would marry him.

Narrow escapes

As a single, wealthy woman, Eleanor was not safe. There were two attempts to kidnap her in the weeks after her divorce. Theobold of Champagne made the first attempt. Warned in time, Eleanor fled under cover of darkness. Henry's younger brother Geoffrey made the second attempt. Again, Eleanor was warned and got away.

Eleanor and Louis were divorced in Aquitaine. It was almost unheard of for a woman to get a divorce—it was a husband's decision—but Eleanor had done it. Louis and the French left Aquitaine, and Eleanor's vassals renewed their allegiance to her. Custody of her daughters, Marie and Alix, was given to their father, as was usual at the time.

Eleanor sent a message to Henry. He came to Aquitaine, where they married secretly. Louis was horrified when he heard. Eleanor had married his most powerful rival. Henry's father had just died and he had now inherited Anjou.

Left: Geoffrey, count of Anjou, the father of Henry, duke of Normandy, Eleanor's second husband.

March 21, 1152
Louis and Eleanor are divorced. Marie and Alix stay with Louis. Eleanor regains control of Aquitaine.

May 18, 1152
Eleanor secretly marries Henry of Anjou, also known as Henry Plantagenet.

Queen of England

Eleanor and her new husband had much in common. They were both ambitious, dynamic, and brave. Their combined lands made them powerful, and Henry had a claim on the English throne. Henry's mother was Matilda, daughter of King Henry I of England. When Matilda's father died in 1135, she was in Anjou and pregnant. This gave King Henry's nephew, Stephen of Blois, the chance to seize the English throne. England was plunged into civil war, but Stephen was victorious.

After he heard about Eleanor and Henry's marriage in May 1152, a furious Louis led an army against Normandy. Henry and his forces responded swiftly and forced Louis to surrender and make a truce. In August, Eleanor and Henry traveled through Aquitaine to meet their vassals.

The Plantagenets

Henry was known as Henry Plantagenet. His nickname came from the sprig of yellow broom he wore in his hat. The plant's Latin name was *planta genista*. The Plantagenets would rule England for more than 300 years.

Above: Eleanor and Henry's sea crossing from France to England was dreadful. There were terrible storms. It took them 24 hours to cross the English Channel. Eleanor was pregnant again, and holding her first son.

January 1153
Henry leaves Eleanor in Aquitaine and invades England. He returns in April 1154 as heir to the English throne.

1153
Eleanor's first son is born. He is baptized William, after the dukes of Aquitaine, and titled count of Poitiers.

Some were suspicious of Henry. When people in Limoges failed to provide enough food for his court, he flew into a terrible rage and ordered the town's walls to be torn down.

Henry left for England with an army to pursue his claim to the throne against Stephen. He left Eleanor in charge of Aquitaine and Anjou. She busied herself granting privileges and money to monasteries and abbeys. While Henry was away, she gave birth to their first son, William.

Henry's English campaigns were successful. He rampaged through England, taking towns and castles, until he confronted King Stephen. Stephen made peace and agreed that Henry would inherit the crown when he died, rather than Stephen's own sons.

Henry returned to Normandy, where Eleanor joined him with their new son. In 1154, news came that Stephen had died. Henry was now the English king, and they prepared to travel to England.

At first, the weather was so bad that they could not sail. Eventually, they made the crossing and went to Winchester, where nobles swore allegiance to Henry. Cheering crowds greeted them at Westminster Abbey in London, where they were crowned king and queen of England.

Left: Westminster Abbey, London, England. Henry and Eleanor were crowned king and queen of England here in great splendor.

1154
Louis VII remarries, to Constance, daughter of Alfonso VII, king of Castile, Spain.

December 19, 1154
Henry and Eleanor are crowned king and queen of England in Westminster Abbey, London.

Affairs of State

Eleanor and Henry now ruled over a huge area. Known as the Angevin empire, it stretched from Scotland to the Pyrenees. Henry's first task as king was to restore peace to England, which had suffered civil war during Stephen's reign. Within a year, he ended rebellions and began to restore law and order. His legal reforms laid the foundation for English common law, which continues to this day.

Henry was always on the move. Like Eleanor's father, he had a traveling court, which moved from one palace or castle to another. He took his treasury and royal officials with him, setting up official courts wherever he stayed. Eleanor often traveled with her husband, bringing their children and members of her own royal household. Henry was often away from England, warring to extend his lands or checking on affairs in Aquitaine, Normandy,

and Anjou. While Henry was away, Eleanor governed England in his name.

Right: A traveling court included horses, wagons, baggage carts, and pack animals, laden with luggage of all kinds. There were at least 200 people in the royal household, all on the move.

February 1155
Eleanor's second son, Henry, is born in London.

1155
Henry makes Thomas Becket chancellor of England. They become close friends.

"God save Lady Eleanor, Queen, who is the arbiter of honor, wit, and beauty, of largesse and loyalty. Lady, born were you in a happy hour and wed to Henry, king."

The poet Philippe de Thaün, about 1154

Henry was the absolute ruler, but Eleanor carried out some official business too—it was very different from her marriage to Louis, when she had had no say in government. Eleanor spent some time in London, but also traveled the country, presiding over courts throughout England, hearing cases, settling disputes, and issuing charters and documents. She was a clever politician and gained a reputation for justice. She also had good financial sense, raising sums of money in her own name and funding a boat dock, called Queenhithe, on the River Thames, to encourage overseas trade. From time to time, she crossed the English Channel to check on her and Henry's lands abroad.

A fair trial
Henry introduced trial by jury in England. Before then, a person had to go through combat or an ordeal to prove his or her innocence of a crime. Before Henry's reforms, if a woman was accused of a crime, such as witchcraft, she had to carry a red-hot iron for three steps. If her skin was burned, she was guilty.

Eleanor encouraged literature and introduced her native troubadour culture throughout their lands. She imported wines from Aquitaine, as well as spices, silks, and exotic goods from the East, which she had discovered in her travels during the crusades. She improved the palace at Westminster, founded nunneries, and gave money to religious institutions, including Fontevrault Abbey in Aquitaine.

1155–56
Eleanor is active in the government of England while Henry is abroad campaigning in Anjou and Maine.

1156
Henry and Eleanor travel to Aquitaine, where Henry puts down rebellious nobles.

Motherhood

A queen was expected to produce sons to continue the family line. Eleanor did this. In the first six years of her marriage to Henry, she had four sons and a daughter—William, Henry, Matilda, Richard, and Geoffrey. Later she also had two more daughters, Eleanor and Joanna, and a final son, John. William died when he was three, but the others survived, which was unusual for a time when many children died from disease.

Above: Isabelle, queen of France, gives birth. Eleanor, like all medieval women, had her babies at home. Ladies-in-waiting were present and a midwife helped with the birth.

Eleanor gave birth in whichever castle she happened to be living in at the time. Poor women breastfed their own children, but noblewomen like Eleanor hired women, called wet nurses, to feed their babies. They were careful who they chose because they believed personality was passed through the milk.

After every birth Eleanor was up and about quickly, traveling on royal business. Often she took babies and nurses with her, but as her children grew, she left them in the care of the royal household. Eleanor bought toys and clothes for her children, but she had little to do with their everyday care.

1158

A royal pageant goes to France to arrange the betrothal of Louis' baby daughter to Eleanor's son, Henry.

1159

Probably encouraged by Eleanor, Henry marches on Toulouse in France but fails to take it.

Eleanor and Henry dreamed of extending their influence. This meant arranging successful marriages, or alliances, for their children. In 1158, Henry arranged for Prince Henry, then only three, to be betrothed to Louis VII's baby daughter, Margaret, from his second marriage. The two children were married in 1160. Henry gained the land of Vexin as a bridal gift, or dowry. However, his hopes of adding France to his empire ended in 1165 when Louis had a son who would inherit his throne. Despite this setback, two of Eleanor's daughters later became queens, and three of her sons became kings. Their descendants included many European kings and queens.

Eleanor's children

Eleanor had 10 children in all, two by Louis and eight by Henry. All her children, except Eleanor and John, died before she did.

By Louis VII:
Marie (1145–98)
Alix (1150–97)

By Henry II:
William (1153–56)
Henry (1155–83)
Matilda (1156–89)
Richard "the Lionheart" (1157–99)
Geoffrey (1158–86)
Eleanor (1161–1214)
Joanna (1165–99)
John "Lackland" (1166–1216)

Below: Medieval boys playing on hobby horses. Sons of the nobility learned to ride, hunt, fight, and joust. They were often sent to other nobles for education. Thomas Becket became Prince Henry's tutor.

1162
Thomas Becket becomes Archbishop of Canterbury.

1165
Louis VII finally has a son, Philip. This ends Henry's hopes of gaining the French crown.

Courtly Love

Below: This image of a pair of lovers comes from *Romance of the Rose*, a French love poem written in the 14th century. In accordance with the rules of courtly love, the lover has to suffer and prove his worth before approaching his lady.

Knights in shining armor, beautiful ladies, tournaments, and daring exploits are all elements of the medieval movement known as "courtly love." The key idea of the movement was pure love, particularly the adoration of a knight for the wife of his lord. Poems and music were written about lovesick knights and beautiful, untouchable ladies. However, it was an idealized picture, quite different from the reality of medieval marriage. But for women such as Eleanor, the ideas of courtly love must have had huge appeal: They showed women as superior, which was new and daring in the Middle Ages.

Courtly love began in Aquitaine in the 11th century. The ideas were made popular by troubadours, like Eleanor's grandfather and Bernard de Ventadour. Eleanor helped to spread courtly love through the courts of medieval Europe. Courtly love was linked to ideals of chivalry, a code of behavior that knights were expected to observe. These ideals included being honorable, loyal, and chaste (not pursuing physical relationships with women outside marriage). Of course, in reality, many knights failed to keep to these rules.

Left: A student declares his love to a noble lady. Courtly love poems and songs often told the stories of young unmarried men who offered their adoration to married noblewomen, knowing they could never be together.

Below: Guinevere, wife of King Arthur, and the knight Sir Lancelot meet and kiss (far left). The legends of King Arthur became popular because they expressed the ideals of chivalry.

"Sweet lady, for your love
With clasped hands, I bless
Your radiance, high above
My deep happiness."

The 12th-century troubadour
Bernard de Ventadour

Separation

In 1166, Eleanor was 44. Her marriage to Henry, which had started so well, was in difficulty. Two years later they separated, and she set up court in Poitiers.

By the late 1160s, Henry's empire was in trouble. Nobles in Aquitaine, Maine, Anjou, and Brittany were rebelling against his rule. Henry had unsuccessfully attacked the Welsh and was quarreling bitterly with his old friend Thomas Becket, who was now Archbishop of Canterbury. Relations with Louis VII were also strained.

Eleanor was not happy in the marriage. Henry had fallen in love with a younger woman, Rosamond Clifford. He had had love affairs before, but Eleanor had ignored them. This time it was too public to ignore.

In addition, Henry was pushing Eleanor away from power and she was no longer a working queen.

Eleanor decided to return to Aquitaine. Diplomatically, she suggested to Henry that her presence in Aquitaine would help to calm rebellions. It suited everyone that Eleanor should return home, so Henry escorted her to Poitiers. Once there, he put down the rebellion brutally.

Gallant knight

In 1168 Eleanor was attacked by nobles in Aquitaine who wanted to punish Henry by taking her hostage. Her knights defended her and she escaped. One knight, William Marshal, was taken hostage. Eleanor paid his ransom. He became a close friend and a tutor for her sons.

1167

Eleanor prepares a lavish *trousseau*— furs, silks, and other fine goods—for her daughter Matilda's wedding.

1168

Eleanor goes to Aquitaine. In 1169, her sons Henry, Richard, and Geoffrey pay homage to Louis VII.

Left: This stained-glass window in Canterbury Cathedral, England, shows Thomas Becket with Henry. Becket's murder shocked the Christian world. Henry was filled with guilt.

He made many noble families destitute, and a few went to seek refuge in France, where Louis offered asylum to Henry's enemies.

Henry left and Eleanor ruled Aquitaine on her own. Poitiers was her home base. Most of her family were with her—Prince Henry and his wife Margaret, her favorite son Richard, Eleanor, Joanna, and Geoffrey with his future wife, Marguerite. Marie, Eleanor's first daughter from her marriage to Louis and now countess of Champagne, may have joined them. Eleanor had not seen Marie for 18 years. Eleanor's vassals were pleased she had returned. She worked hard to restore peace, ruling the duchy calmly and efficiently.

Eleanor turned Poitiers into a glittering cultural center once again. Troubadours, musicians, poets, knights, and noble ladies flocked to her court. There were feasts, festivals, and tournaments—mock battles between mounted knights—which young Henry and Richard loved. Eleanor met up with her husband on various occasions but they never lived together again.

Thomas Becket

Henry made his chancellor Thomas Becket Archbishop of Canterbury. As chancellor, Becket's first loyalty was to Henry. As archbishop, his first loyalty was to God. The two close friends quarreled for many years. Finally, in 1170, four of Henry's officers murdered Becket. Henry became the most hated man in Europe, while Becket was canonized (made a saint) in 1173.

1170
Eleanor makes her son Richard her heir and has him made duke of Aquitaine in a spectacular ceremony.

December 29, 1170
Thomas Becket is murdered in Canterbury Cathedral, England.

PRISONER AND
STATESWOMAN

4

Rebellion and Betrayal

Between 1173 and 1174, Eleanor's eldest sons—Henry, Richard, and Geoffrey—rebelled against their father with her support. The king crushed their rebellion and took Eleanor prisoner.

Previous page: When Eleanor was nearly 70 she crossed the Alps (shown here) on horseback into Italy. She crossed the Pyrenees when she was 78.

Below: This mural, which is in the chapel at Chinon, was discovered in 1964. It may show Eleanor (center) being led away by King Henry (far right), or it may be Eleanor with Richard. No one is certain.

From the start of the 1170s, Eleanor devoted herself to her children's interests. Her eldest sons lived with her in Poitiers and had little respect for their father. They were teenagers—an age considered adult in medieval times—but had no power. Their father had decided their inheritance: Henry was duke of Normandy and Anjou and heir to the English throne; Richard was duke of Aquitaine; and Geoffrey was count of Brittany.

March 1173

Prince Henry escapes from Chinon and seeks support from Louis in France. Eleanor follows and is captured.

May 1173

Princes Henry and Richard invade Normandy, while Louis and Geoffrey attack the Vexin.

But their father continued to control the empire. Young Henry was not even allowed to rule England while his father was away.

Eleanor's sons grew resentful and Eleanor sided with them. In meetings with King Henry, she argued their case unsuccessfully. Behind his back, she started to plot against him. She approached her ex-husband, Louis, for his support, as well as her own vassals, who were keen to rebel against Henry's heavy-handed control.

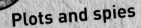

Plots and spies

Some chroniclers (medieval historians) believed Eleanor planned the rebellion—others did not. But all agreed that she played a major role. Henry was shocked by her treachery. He may have placed spies in Poitiers, which is how he learned she was trying to escape and managed to capture her.

Hearing rumors, King Henry decided to keep his eye on the young Prince Henry and took him to Chinon. Young Henry escaped to France, where Louis agreed to join him in an attack on his father. Richard and Geoffrey followed. Henry knew Eleanor was involved and believed she and her court were turning his sons against him. She left Poitiers, disguised as a knight, to follow her sons, but was captured by Henry's men and put under guard.

In May 1173, war broke out. Eleanor's sons, with Louis and nobles throughout the Angevin lands, rose up against Henry. There were rebellions in England, and the Scottish king invaded—Henry was attacked on all sides. He gathered a huge force of mercenaries (paid soldiers) and counter-attacked. He moved speedily to put down the uprisings, attacked Poitiers, and broke up Eleanor's court. In July 1174, he took Eleanor to England and imprisoned her. He besieged Rouen and forced his sons and Louis to surrender. Henry made peace with his sons, but Eleanor stayed in prison.

September–November 1173
King Henry invades Poitiers. His forces suppress rebellions. A truce is called, then fighting begins again in spring 1174.

July 1174
Eleanor is imprisoned in Old Sarum Castle, Salisbury, England.

Prison and Loss

Eleanor was taken as prisoner to Old Sarum Castle at Salisbury, England. She was not locked up in a cell like a criminal—she could wander the castle freely. But she was cut off from family and friends, and was always under guard. It was a stark contrast to her previous life.

Henry did not know what to do about Eleanor. He suggested that they divorce and she go into a nunnery, as abbess of Fontevrault Abbey in Aquitaine, but Eleanor refused. She was not ready to disappear from the world completely.

Eleanor was still a queen, and from time to time she was allowed out, under guard. In 1176 she went to Winchester to help her youngest daughter, Joanna, prepare for marriage to the king of Sicily.

Below: When Eleanor was first captured she was taken to Henry's castle at Chinon. She was here for some months before being taken to England.

1175
Eleanor rejects divorce and Henry's suggestion that she retire to Fontevrault Abbey.

1180
Eleanor's first husband, Louis VII, dies. His son Philip succeeds him as king of France.

Left: A seal showing Henry II sitting on his throne. He was not prepared to share power with his sons—he was an absolute ruler and did not trust their ability to rule.

Henry's eldest sons continued to plot against their father. Henry now favored his youngest son, John. He kept him close and angered the others by giving him lands belonging to them. In 1180, Eleanor's first husband, Louis, died. His son Philip became king of France and was determined to break the power of the Plantagenets.

Prince Henry died of dysentery in 1183. On his deathbed he pleaded for Eleanor's release. In November 1184, Henry summoned Eleanor to Westminster to discuss their sons' inheritance. She was now 62 and still beautiful, graceful, and clever. Henry wanted Eleanor to persuade Richard to give Aquitaine to John, his favorite. There was a fierce row, and Eleanor refused. Two years later, Geoffrey died, trampled to death by a horse.

Henry was tired and seriously ill. His eldest surviving son, Richard, and King Philip of France had joined forces. They demanded Henry give up his lands and recognize Richard as king of England. Henry was upset when he learned that Prince John, his favorite, had also plotted against him. Shortly afterwards, Henry died. Eleanor was free once more.

Dream of death

When a messenger arrived to tell Eleanor of her son Henry's death, she said that she had foreseen his death in a dream. She dreamed he was lying on a couch, wearing two crowns. One was his solid gold crown, the other was of brilliant light. She knew her son had died and gone to heaven.

June 11, 1183
Eleanor's eldest son, Prince Henry, dies. Three years later, her third son, Geoffrey, is killed.

July 6, 1189
Henry II dies and is buried at Fontevrault Abbey.

Queen Regent

Eleanor was free and her beloved son, Richard, was king. She devoted herself to his interests, ruling wisely in his absence and preventing his brother John from seizing the throne.

Despite 15 years as a prisoner, Eleanor was as energetic and determined as ever. After his father's death, Richard stayed in Normandy settling his affairs. Eleanor paved the way for Richard's kingship, visiting great lords and receiving their oaths of allegiance on his behalf. She prepared a spectacular coronation for Richard, which took place in Westminster Abbey.

Less than a year after his coronation, Richard raised large sums of money and left on the Third Crusade with King Philip of France.

Knowing Richard had no heir, Eleanor arranged a marriage for Richard with a Spanish noblewoman called Berengaria of Navarre.

Left: Richard I (1157–99), named "the Lionheart" for his bravery, was Eleanor's favorite son. He was brave and handsome, but could be very brutal.

September 3, 1189

Richard is crowned king of England. He leaves on the Third Crusade the following year.

1190

Eleanor collects Berengaria, Richard's bride to be, and takes her to Sicily, reaching Richard before his departure.

Eleanor took Berengaria to Sicily to join Richard before he left for the Holy Land. Berengaria and Richard married but rarely lived together and had no children.

Eleanor settled in Normandy, ruling Richard's kingdom while he was away. She undid some of Henry's harsh laws and released prisoners. As she feared, John made two attempts to seize the throne. Philip of France, who returned early from the crusade, supported John. Each time, Eleanor moved swiftly. She roused support, prevented the invasions, and kept the throne safe for Richard.

In 1193, Eleanor heard that Richard had been captured on his way back from the crusade by the German emperor, Henry VI. Eleanor raised Richard's ransom and took it to Germany. Back in England, Richard was greeted as a conquering hero. He had won the cities of Jaffa and Acre from the Muslims, but had failed to capture Jerusalem.

An incredible journey

Eleanor was almost 70 when she crossed the Pyrenees to Navarre to collect Berengaria. She traveled back over the Pyrenees on horseback with the young princess and a small escort, then through the Alps into Italy, down the western coast, and by boat to Sicily, where they met up with Richard. After only four days' rest, she made the return journey. Her round trip was an extraordinary 2,500 miles (4,000 km).

In 1194, Eleanor and Richard went to live in their Angevin lands across the English Channel. Eleanor never returned to England. She persuaded John and Richard to make peace, and then retired to the Fontevrault Abbey. Philip continued to wage war against Richard. In 1199, Richard was wounded in France. Knowing that he was dying, Richard made John his heir. Eleanor rushed from Fontevrault and was with her son when he died.

1193–94
Eleanor raises Richard's ransom of 150,000 silver marks, equal to 35 tons of silver.

1199
Richard dies of a battle wound. John succeeds him as king of England.

Women and the Church

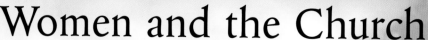

Below: The beautiful Fontevrault Abbey on the River Loire, close to Poitiers. A mystic and scholar called Robert d'Arbrissel founded the abbey. He believed that women were, in many ways, superior to men. Many aristocratic women spent time at Fontevrault.

In the Middle Ages, women who wanted to devote their lives to religion became nuns and went to live in religious communities called nunneries. Women were not allowed to be priests and perform religious services for a congregation. Nuns spent their time praying, working, and studying. They were also healers who cared for the sick. The woman who ran the abbey was called an abbess. Most nuns were noble-born women, and many, such as Hildegard of Bingen (1098–1179), a German abbess, were very well educated. Nunneries were often places of great learning. For many women, the religious life gave them education and control over their own lives. Some abbesses became powerful leaders. Eleanor, like other members of the nobility and royalty, donated large sums of money to religious houses. Her favorite religious house was the Abbey of Fontevrault. It was founded in 1100 with money provided by her grandfather, William IX. Eleanor granted the abbey special privileges and donated money. She went to live there in her old age.

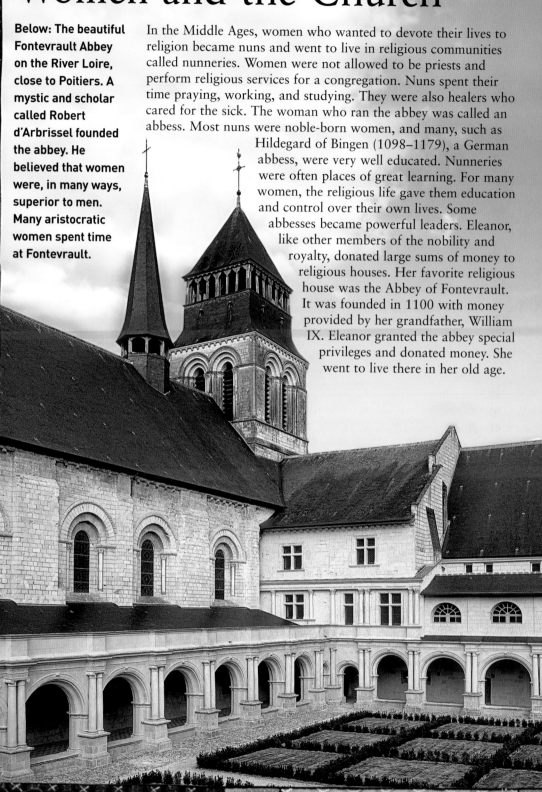

Above: This 15th-century illustrated manuscript shows rows of nuns in choir stalls. Their black robes were called habits. The white cloth on their heads and necks was called a wimple.

A NUN'S LIFE

Single women who could not marry, or did not want to, often entered a nunnery. Sometimes, widowed women became nuns, or women entered to escape a violent husband. Noble families sent young daughters into nunneries to be educated or train for a religious life.

Death and Legacy

With Richard dead, Eleanor worked to support John. He was her least favorite son, but Richard had named him heir to the English throne as well as to Aquitaine, Normandy, and Anjou. But there was another claimant to the throne: her grandson, Arthur, who was Geoffrey's son. Arthur was in league with King Philip of France.

Eleanor was now 77. She set off on a grand tour of Aquitaine to prepare the way for John. In her wish for peace, and to ensure loyalty to John, she even did homage to Philip, king of France. In three months, she covered more than 1,000 miles (1,600 km). In a further effort to ensure peace, Eleanor arranged for her granddaughter, Blanche, to marry Prince Louis, the grandson of her former husband, Louis.

In 1202, however, war broke out. John had angered Philip who, together with Arthur, launched an attack. Arthur marched on Aquitaine and besieged Eleanor in Mirabeau castle. Eleanor managed to hold out until John arrived to rescue her. Exhausted, Eleanor returned to Fontevrault Abbey, where she died on April 1, 1204. Soon after her death, Normandy and Anjou fell to the French, but Aquitaine stayed under Plantagenet control for another 200 years.

> "*She enhanced the grandeur of her birth by the honesty of her life... she surpassed [bettered] almost all the queens of the world.*"
> **Nuns of Fontevrault on the death of Eleanor of Aquitaine**

May 25, 1199
Eleanor's son, John, is crowned at Westminster Abbey, London.

1200
Eleanor travels to Castile to collect her granddaughter Blanche.

Final journey

In 1200, Eleanor made a final, remarkable journey, traveling over the Pyrenees into Spain. It was January and there were storms and sleet. She arrived in Castile, where she met up with her daughter and namesake, Eleanor, for the first time in 30 years. Eleanor chose her granddaughter, Blanche, to marry Louis, prince of France. It was a wise choice. Blanche became a great queen.

Eleanor was an extraordinary woman. She was a headstrong girl who became a wise stateswoman. Married to two kings, she played a major role in political events, which was unusual for women of that time. Through diplomacy and clever alliances she helped to create an empire. She was criticized for troublemaking, but she was brave and independent. She remains one of history's most impressive queens.

Below: The tomb effigies of Eleanor and Henry II of England in Fontevrault Abbey. Eleanor was 82 when she died—a remarkable age for the time.

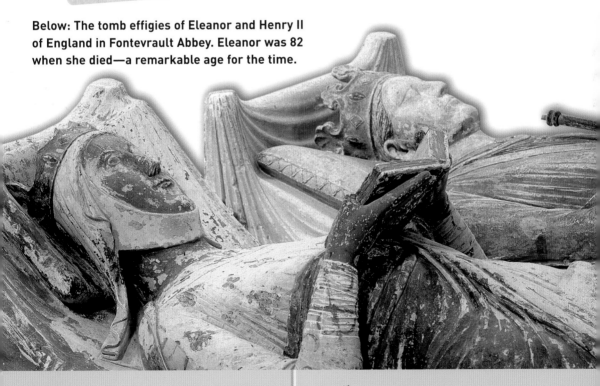

1202
Eleanor's grandson Arthur besieges her in Mirabeau. John rescues her and imprisons, or possibly kills, Arthur.

April 1, 1204
Eleanor dies and is buried at Fontevrault Abbey, together with Henry II and her son Richard.

Glossary

abbess the highest-ranking woman in an abbey.

allegiance loyalty toward a ruler.

Amazons in ancient Greek myths, the Amazons were a race of fierce women warriors.

Angevin Empire the name given to Henry II's empire which was centered on the town of Anjou.

baron a nobleman of any rank.

besiege to surround a castle or town in order to force the inhabitants to surrender.

betrothed to be engaged to be married.

broom a small shrub with yellow flowers.

Byzantine Empire the eastern part of the Roman Empire, created when the Roman Empire collapsed. It lasted from A.D. 330 to 1453.

charter document issued by a king or queen granting rights to a person or organization.

chivalry the rules of behavior followed by knights and nobles in medieval Europe.

cleric a religious official.

conjurer an entertainer who performs magic tricks.

count a nobleman who ranks below a duke.

county in medieval times, an area ruled by a count.

courtly love a medieval movement that idealized a knight's pure love for a noblewoman, who was usually married.

crusades military expeditions made by European Christians in the Middle Ages to take the Holy Land from Muslims.

destitute without money, food, or shelter.

domain an area of land controlled by a ruler or royal family.

dowry the money and property that a woman or her parents give her husband on the marriage.

duchy in medieval times, an area ruled by a duke. It could be independent of a king if the duke was very powerful.

duke a nobleman of the highest rank below that of a prince.

effigy a carved figure of someone, which is usually found on a tomb.

excommunicate to expel or throw someone out of the Roman Catholic Church.

fealty an oath of loyalty to a superior, such as a lord, duke, or king.

feudalism a term used to describe the system of landholding in medieval Europe. Tenants held land granted by kings or lords in exchange for military service.

fief the land given by the king to nobles in exchange for military service.

heir a person who can legally inherit property or a title from someone when that person dies.

Holy Land part of the ancient Middle East. Today, the area includes Jordan and Israel.

homage a show of loyalty. A medieval knight did homage to his lord by placing his hands in the palms of his lord. In exchange, the knight received a kiss of peace.

jongleur a word of French origin which means juggler, or entertainer.

keep the central tower inside the walls of a medieval fortress or castle.

litter a couch suspended on poles and carried on people's shoulders or by horses.

marionette a type of puppet that is controlled by strings.

medieval relating to the Middle Ages.

Middle Ages a time in European history between the fifth century and the mid-1400s.

moat water that surrounds a castle.

noble someone belonging to the aristocratic class, with social privileges and power.

overlord a ruler, such as a king, who holds power over lesser rulers, such as counts.

penance a punishment willingly undergone after committing a sin.

petition a formal request.

pilgrimage a religious journey made to a sacred place, such as a shrine.

privilege a right or benefit granted by a ruler to a person or organization.

Provençal a language that was spoken in southern France in the Middle Ages.

ramparts the fortified walls that surround a castle or fortress.

regent a person who governs a territory when the king or queen is away or unable to do so, for a reason such as illness.

retinue people who follow and serve an important person, such as a king or duke.

rushes grass-like plants whose leaves can be dried and were once used to cover a floor instead of a carpet.

scribe a person who copies manuscripts or writes out documents.

sprig a small shoot or piece of a plant.

stateswoman a respected leader who is devoted to public service; also statesman.

tabor a small medieval drum.

tournament a competition between knights fighting on horseback with lances and shields or on foot with swords, maces, and shields.

troubadour poet who wrote and sang verses about love.

trousseau clothing and personal possessions collected for a bride.

vassal in the feudal system, a powerful lord who received land from the king in return for an oath of loyalty and a promise to provide military service.

witness declare a document to be correct and valid by signing it.

Bibliography

Weir, Alison, *Eleanor of Aquitaine: By the Wrath of God, Queen of England*, Pimlico, London, 2000

Eyewitness Guide: Medieval Life, Dorling Kindersley, London, 1996

History in Writing: The Crusades, Evens Brothers, London, 1999

Schoyer Brooks, Polly, *Queen Eleanor: Independent Spirit of the Medieval World*, Houghton Mifflin, Boston, 1983

Eastwood, Kay, *Women and Girls in the Middle Ages*, Crabtree, Ontario, 2004

Sources of quotes:

p.33 *Eleanor of Aquitaine: By the Wrath of God, Queen of England*, Alison Weir, p.19

p.41 *Eleanor of Aquitaine: By the Wrath of God, Queen of England*, Alison Weir, p.132

p.45 *Queen Eleanor: Independent Spirit of the Medieval World*, Polly Schoyer Brooks, p.67

p.58 *Queen Eleanor: Independent Spirit of the Medieval World*, Polly Schoyer Brooks, p.164

Some Web sites that will help you to explore Eleanor of Aquitaine's world:

www.royalty.nu/Europe/England/Angevin/Eleanor.html

www.womeninworldhistory.com/heroine2.html

en.wikipedia.org/wiki/Eleanor_of_Aquitaine

library.thinkquest.org/12834/text/sistercities.html

www.yourchildlearns.com/castle_history.htm

mw.mcmaster.ca/timeline.html

Index

Acknowledgments

AA = The Art Archive, BAL = The Bridgeman Art Library, SHP = Sonia Halliday Photographs.

B = bottom, C = center, T = top, L = left, R = right.

Front cover Statue of Eleanor at Chartres Cathedral/SHP; **1** AA/Bibliothèque Municipale, Dijon/Dagli Orti; **3** John Parker; **4T** BAL/Musée Condé, Chantilly; **4B** akg-images; **5T, 5B** John Parker; **7, 8** BAL/Musée Condé, Chantilly; **9** Corbis/© Ric Ergenbright; **11** John Parker; **12, 13T** SHP; **13CR** SHP/Bibliothèque Nationale, Paris; **13L** BAL/Bibliothèque Nationale, Paris; **14** AA/British Library, London; **15** BAL/Bibliothèque Municipale, Dijon; **16** AA/Bibliothèque Universitaire de Mèdecine, Montpellier/Dagli Orti; **17** AA/Victoria and Albert Museum, London/Graham Brandon; **19** akg-images; **20** BAL/Bibliothèque Nationale, Paris; **21** BAL/Musée Condé, Chantilly; **22** AA/Bibliothèque Municipale, Castres/Dagli Orti; **23** Scala, Florence/British Library, London; **24** John Parker; **25** BAL/Louvre, Paris; **26** SHP; **27** John Parker; **28** BAL/Bibliothèque Nationale, Paris; **29T** SHP/Bibliothèque Nationale, Paris; **29B** Scala, Florence; **30** BAL/Bibliothèque Nationale, Paris; **31** AA/Basilica San Marco, Venice/Dagli Orti; **32** BAL/Bibliothèque Nationale, Paris; **35** John Parker; **36** akg-images/British Library, London; **37** AA/Musée de Tessé, Le Mans/Dagli Orti; **38** John Parker; **39** Getty Images/Stone; **40** BAL/British Library, London; **42** BAL/Bibliothèque Municipale, Boulogne-sur-Mer; **43** AA/Bodleian Library, Oxford; **44, 44–45** AA/British Library, London; **45T** AA/Bibliothèque Universitaire de Mèdecine, Montpellier/Dagli Orti; **45B** Scala, Florence/British Library, London; **47** SHP; **49, 50, 52** John Parker; **53** AA/British Library, London; **54** Scala Florence/British Library, London; **56** John Parker; **57T** Scala, Florence/British Library, London; **57BR** AA/Bodleian Library, Oxford; **59** John Parker.